newwoman

Bloke Jokes 3

THIS IS A CARLTON BOOK

This edition published by Carlton Books Limited 2003
20 Mortimer Street
London W1T 3JW

A CIP catalogue for this book is available from the British Library.

ISBN 1 84442 957 1

Executive Editor: Roland Hall
Senior Art Editor: Diane Spender
Editor: Louise Johnson
Design: Addition
Production: Lisa Moore
Illustrations: Sarah Nayler

NeWwoman

Edited by **Louise Johnson**

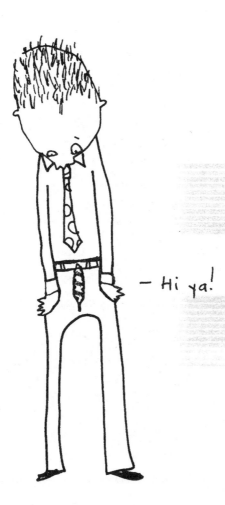

– Hi ya!

Bloke Jokes 3

... because men are still funny

CONTENTS

1

GREAT MYSTERIES OF OUR TIME (I)

WHAT'S ALL THAT ABOUT?

What do you give **the bloke** who has everything?

Penicillin.

What happens when a bloke eats a mosquito?

He has more brain cells in his stomach than his head.

What do you get when you offer a bloke a penny for his thoughts?

Change.

What's the thickest **book** in the world?

What Blokes Think They Know About Women.

What do you get when four **blokes** go fishing together and one comes back after catching nothing?

Three Men And A Baby.

What do you never **want to hear while having great sex?**

Honey, I'm home!

What do you call an attractive, intelligent and sensitive man?

A rumour.

What's the difference between a man and a yoghurt?

A yoghurt has culture!

What happened when the woman put an ad in the classifieds saying 'Husband wanted'?

Next day she received a hundred letters all saying: 'You can have mine.'

What's the best revenge when a woman steals your bloke?

Let her keep him.

What's the definition of a wedding tragedy?

Marrying a bloke for love, and then finding out he has no money.

What is the proof that the average woman can take a joke?

The average bloke.

What do you do with a bloke who thinks he's God's gift to women?

Take him back and exchange him.

What happens when a woman makes a fool of a bloke?

It's usually an improvement.

What do you see when you look into a bloke's eyes?

The back of his head.

What's the difference between Bigfoot and an intelligent bloke?

Bigfoot's been spotted several times.

What do most blokes consider a gourmet restaurant?

Any place without a drive-up window.

What's the best place to hide a bloke's birthday present?

The washing basket.

What's the difference between a bloke with a mid-life crisis and a clown?

A clown knows he's
wearing funny clothes.

What's easier to make, a snowman or a snowwoman?

A snowwoman – because with
a snowman you have to hollow
out the head and use all that extra
snow to make its **testicles**.

What's the difference between a bloke and Bigfoot?

One is covered with
matted hair and **smells awful**.
The other has big feet.

What's a bloke's idea of foreplay?

**Prodding you
to see if
you're awake.**

What's the difference between a bald bloke and a bloke with hair?

One's got no hair.

What's the difference between a cow chewing the cud, and a bloke chewing gum?

The intelligent look
on the cow's face.

What can you say to a bloke who's just had sex?

Anything you like – he's asleep!

What's a bloke's idea of helping to make the bed?

Getting out of it.

What's a bloke's definition of 'conflict of interest'?

When pizza
arrives during sex.

What's a bloke's idea of helping around the house?

Dropping his
clothes where you
can pick them up.

What's a bloke's definition of recycling?

Using beer cans as ashtrays before throwing them on the side of the road.

2

EVERYONE LIKES A LIST, DON'T THEY?

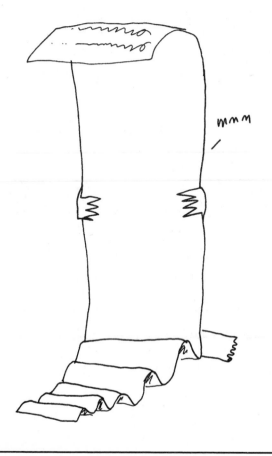

How to Tell Someone Their Fly Is Unzipped...

- You've got your fly set for 'Monica' instead of 'Hillary.'

- You've got Windows on your laptop.

- Quasimodo needs to go back in the tower and tend to his bells.

- Paging Mr. Johnson... Paging Mr. Johnson...

- Your pod bay door is open, Hal.

- Elvis Junior has left the building!

- Mini Me is making a break for fame.

- Ensign Hanes is reporting a hull breach on the lower deck, Sir!

- Captain, sensors detect a wormhole in the forward quadrant!

- Sailor Ned's trying to take a little shore leave.

- Your dork is ajar.

- You've got a security breach at Los Pantalones.

- I see you have an opening in senior management.

- Our next guest is someone who needs no introduction.

– Hi ya!

The Eight Qualities Of A Perfect Husband

- **B**rave

- **I**ntelligent

- **G**entle

- **P**olite

- **E**nergetic

- **N**utty

- **I**ndustrious

- **S**ensitive

**And if all else fails, well...
read the CAPITAL LETTERS only**

New chemical element

Element name: Man

Symbol: XY **Atomic weight**: (180 +/-50)

Physical properties: Solid at room temperature, but gets bent out of shape easily. Fairly dense and sometimes flaky. Difficult to find a pure sample. Due to rust, ageing samples are unable to conduct electricity as easily as young samples.

Chemical properties: Attempts to bond with WO (Element: woman) any chance it can get. Also tends to form strong bonds with itself. Becomes explosive when mixed with KD (Element: child) for prolonged period of time. Neutralise by saturating with alcohol.

Usage: None known. Possibly good source of methane. Good specimens are able to produce large quantities on command.

Caution: In the absence of WO, this element rapidly decomposes and begins to smell.

Evening classes for blokes

- The Gas Gauge In Your Car: Sometimes Empty **MEANS** Empty.

- Dressing Up: Beyond the Funeral and the Wedding

- Going To The Supermarket: It's Not Just For Women Anymore!

- Giving Back To The Community: How To Donate 15-Year-Old Levis To Oxfam.

- Romance: More Than A Cable Channel!

- Directions: It's Okay To Ask for Them.

- Strange But True: She Really May NOT Care What The Offside Trap Is About.

- 'I Could Have Played a Better Game Than That!': Why Women Laugh.

- 'I Don't Know': Be The First Bloke To Say It!

Put downs for blokes who really deserve them:

• Are those your eyeballs? I found them in my cleavage.

• Did the aliens forget to remove your anal probe?

• Whatever kind of look you were going for, you missed.

• It ain't the size, it's… no, it's the size.

• I'm trying to imagine you with a personality.

• Too many freaks, not enough circuses.

• Nice aftershave. Must you marinate in it?

• And which dwarf are you?

• If I want to hear the pitter patter of little feet, I'll put shoes on my cats.

• Did I mention the kick in the groin you'll be receiving if you touch me?

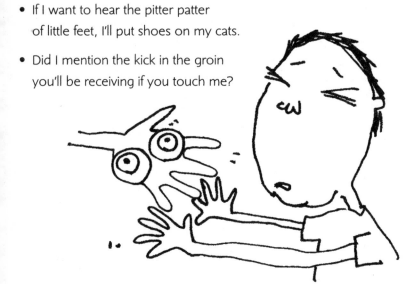

Condom mania

Imagine if all major retailers started making their own condoms and keeping the same tagline…

Polo condoms – the condom with the hole!!! (VERY poor seller!!!).

Sainsbury's Condoms – making life taste better.

Abbey National condoms – because life is complicated enough.

Pringles condoms – once you pop, you can't stop.

Burger King condoms – Home of the whopper.

Goodyear condoms – 'for a longer ride go wide.'

Renault condoms – size really does matter!

Domestos condoms – get right under the rim!

Why are blokes just dogs without the fur?

- They spend all day sprawled on the most comfortable piece of furniture in the house.

- They can hear food opening half a mile away, but don't hear you when you're in the same room.

- They can look dumb and lovable all at the same time.

- They growl when they're not happy.

- When you want to play, they want to play.

- When you want to be alone, they want to play.

- They leave their toys everywhere.

- They do disgusting things with their mouths and then try to give you a kiss!

- They go right to your crotch as soon as they meet you.

Blokespeak (phrasebook for the opposite sex)

- 'Haven't I seen you before?'   *translation*   **'Nice ass.'**
- 'I'm a Romantic.'   *translation*   **'I'm poor'**
- 'I need you'   *translation*   **'My hand is tired'**

Five secrets of a perfect relationship

1 It is important to find a man who
   helps at home, who cooks from time
   to time, who cleans up and who has a job.

2 It is important to find a man
   who can ***make you laugh***.

3 It is important to find a man who you
   can trust and who ***doesn't lie*** to you.

4 It is important to find a man who is
   good in bed and who likes to be with you.

*****

5 It is very important that these
   four men ***don't know each other***.

Things that are difficult for blokes to say when they're drunk:

- Innovative.

- Preliminary.

- Proliferation.

- Cinnamon.

Things that are VERY difficult for blokes to say when they're drunk:

- Specificity.

- British Constitution.

- Passive-aggressive disorder.

- Transubstantiate.

Things that are Downright Impossible for blokes to say when they're drunk:

- Thanks, but I don't want to sleep with you.

- Nope, no more booze for me.

- Sorry, but you're not really my type.

- No kebab for me, thank you.

- Good evening officer, isn't it a lovely evening.

- Oh, I just couldn't – no-one wants to hear me sing.

- No, I won't make any attempt to dance thanks,
  I have zero coordination.

A two-year degree is being offered at Life University that many of you should be interested in: **Becoming A Real Bloke**. That's right, in just six terms, you, too, can be a real bloke.

Please take a moment to look over the program outline.

FIRST YEAR

Autumn Term:

- MEN 101 Combating Stupidity

- MEN 102 You, Too, Can Do Housework

- MEN 103 PMS – Learn When To Keep Your Mouth Shut

- MEN 104 We Do Not Want Sleazy Underthings For Christmas

Winter Term:

- MEN 110 Wonderful Laundry Techniques

- MEN 111 Understanding The Female Response To Getting In At 4am

- MEN 112 Parenting: It Doesn't End With Conception

- EAT 100 Get A Life, Learn To Cook

- EAT 101 Get A Life, Learn To Cook II

- ECON 001A What's Hers Is Hers

Spring Term:

- MEN 120 How NOT To Act Like An Arse When You're Wrong

- MEN 121 Understanding Your Incompetence

- MEN 122 YOU, The Weaker Sex

- MEN 123 Reasons To Give Flowers

SECOND YEAR

Autumn Term:

- SEX 101 You CAN Fall Asleep Without It

- SEX 102 Morning Dilemma: If It's Awake, Take A Shower

- MEN 201 How To Stay Awake After Sex

- MEN 202 How To Put the Toilet Seat Down – Optional
  (See other options below)

Winter Term:

- MEN 210 The Remote Control: Overcoming Your Dependency

- MEN 211 How To Not Act Younger Than Your Children

- MEN 212 You, Too, Can Be A Designated Driver

- MEN 213 Honest, You Don't Look Like Tom Cruise,
  Especially When Naked

- MEN 230A Her Birthdays And Anniversaries Are Important

Spring Term:

- MEN 220 Omitting %&*! From Your Vocabulary (Pass/Fail Only)

- MEN 221 Fluffing The Blanket After Farting Is Not Necessary

- MEN 222 Real Blokes Ask For Directions

- MEN 223 Thirty Minutes Of Begging Is NOT Considered Foreplay

- MEN 230B Her Birthdays And Anniversaries Are Important II

Course Options:

- EAT 101 Cooking With Tofu

- EAT 102 Utilisation Of Eating Utensils

- EAT 103 Burping And Belching Discreetly

- MEN 231 Mothers-in-law

- MEN 232 Appear To Be Listening

- MEN 233 Just Say 'Yes, Dear'

- ECON 001B Cheaper To Keep Her (Must Pass ECON 001A)

3

DOCTOR, DOCTOR...

Did you hear about the bloke who mistook Viagra for his sleeping tablets?

He woke up with a stiff neck.

An 88-year-old woman goes to the doctor for Viagra for her **90-year-old** husband. The bemused doctor asks whether she wants regular, strong or extra potent tablets. When she replied 'regular' the doctor queried her choice because of her husband's advanced age, suggesting that **'extra strong'** might be more suitable. 'Oh, it's not for that,' the wife replied, a little embarrassed. 'I just want him to stop **peeing on his feet**!'

A bloke returns from the doctor and tells his wife that he's been given just **24 hours to live**. Given this prognosis, he asks his wife for sex. Naturally, she agrees, and they make love.

About six hours later, the bloke goes to his wife and says, 'Honey, you know I now have only **18 hours to live**. Could we please do it one more time?'

Of course, the wife agrees and they do it again. Later, as the bloke gets into bed, he looks at his watch and realises that he now has only 8 hours left.

He touches his wife's shoulder and asks, 'Honey, please... just one more time before I die.' She says, 'Of course, dear.' And they **make love for the third time**. After this session, the wife rolls over and falls asleep.

The bloke, however, worried about his impending death, tosses and turns until he's down to **4 more hours**. He taps his wife, who rouses. 'Honey, I have only 4 more hours. Do you think we could...'

At this point the wife sits up and says, 'Listen honey, I have to get up in the morning, **you don't**.'

A bloke with a winking problem is applying for a position as a sales representative for a large firm. The interviewer is bowled over: 'This is phenomenal. You've graduated from the best schools; your recommendations are wonderful and your experience is unparalleled. Normally, we'd hire you without a second thought, but we're afraid your constant winking might scare off potential customers.' 'Wait,' says the bloke. 'If I take two aspirin, I'll stop winking!' He reaches into his jacket pocket and begins pulling out all sorts of **condoms**: red, blue, ribbed, flavoured; finally, at the bottom, he finds a packet of aspirin and after swallowing two he stops winking in a few moments. 'That's all well and good,' says the interviewer. 'But this is a respectable company, we can't have our **employees womanising** all over the country!'

'What do you mean?' says the bloke. 'I'm a happily married man!'

'So how do you **explain all these condoms?**'

'Oh, that,' he sighed. 'Have you ever walked into a pharmacy, **winking**, and asked for aspirin?'

An eighty-year-old bloke was having an annual **physical**. As the doctor was listening to his heart with the stethoscope, he began muttering, 'Oh oh!'

The bloke asked the doctor what the problem was.

'Well,' said the doc, 'You have a serious heart murmur. Do you smoke?'

'No,' replied the bloke.

'Do you **drink in excess**?'

'No,' replied the bloke.

'Do you have a **sex life**?'

'Yes, I do!'

'Well,' said the doc, 'I'm afraid with this heart murmur, you'll have to **give up half your sex life**.'

Looking perplexed, the old bloke said, 'Which half – the looking or the thinking?'

And what about the new **Viagra** eyedrops? They're not much good for your eyes, they just make blokes look **hard**.

A bloke goes to the doctor with a piece of lettuce **sticking out of his bum**. He tells the doctor he's a little concerned, and asks for an examination.

After a **little probing**, the doctor turns to his patient and says 'It's worse than I originally thought – that's just the tip of the iceberg.'

B lokes beware – it's been revealed that criminals who steal Viagra will face **stiff** sentencing.

A bloke goes to the doctors and says: 'Doctor, every time I sneeze **I have an orgasm**.'

The doctor says: 'What are you taking for it?'

And the bloke replies: **'Pepper!'**

There's a new drink on the market today. It is called Viagraccino – one cup and you're up all night.

A bloke is in a terrible accident, and his '**manhood**' is mangled and torn from his body. His doctor assures him that modern medicine could replace it but that his insurance wouldn't cover the surgery, since it was considered cosmetic. The doctor gives him three quotes: £3,500 for **small**, £6,500 for **medium**, and £14,000 for **large**. The bloke was pretty sure he wanted a large, but the doctor urged him to talk it over with his wife before he made any decision. So the bloke leaves the room to call his wife to explain their options, but returns looking very dejected. 'Well, what have the two of you decided?' asks the doctor. The bloke answers: 'She'd rather have a new kitchen.'

Doctor, you've got to help me,' says the bloke on the couch. 'Every night I have the same **horrible dream**. I'm lying in bed when all of a sudden five women rush in and start tearing off my clothes.'

The psychiatrist nods. 'And what do you do when this happens?'

'I push them away,' says the bloke.

'I, see,' replies the psychiatrist. 'And what do you want me to do?'

'Break my arms!'

This bloke's been having a few **'arousal' problems** and goes to see a **private doctor** who prescribes **Viagra**. Armed with the prescription he goes with his wife to the chemist and is shocked to find that the price is £10 per pill. 'Oh well,' says his wife. '£40 a year isn't too bad!'

A bloke goes to see his doctor for his test results, and things are looking really grim. 'I'm sorry,' says the doctor, 'but you only have three minutes to live.'

'Surely there must be something you can do for me?' begs the bloke.

'Well,' says the doctor. **'I could boil you an egg...'**

4

GREAT MYSTERIES OF OUR TIME (II) – HOW COME?

How do you make 7 pounds of fat look attractive to a bloke?

Put a nipple on it.

How do most blokes define marriage?

A very expensive way of getting their laundry done free.

How do blokes know when the clocks have gone back?

When their 5 o'clock shadow appears at 4 o'clock.

How do you make a bloke's eyes light up?

Shine a torch in his ear.

How does a man show that he is planning for the future?

He buys **two** cases of beer.

How do you tell if your bloke's died during sex?

He stays **stiff** for longer than two minutes.

How can you tell if a bloke has a small penis, without touching or looking?

Check out the sports car in his driveway.

How stupid are blokes about money?

Only a man would buy a £500 car and put a £4,000 stereo in it.

**How can you tell that
soap operas are fictional?**

In real life, blokes
aren't affectionate
in bed.

**How is being at a singles bar
different to being at the circus?**

At the circus, the
clowns don't talk.

How do blokes' braincells die?

Alone.

How do blokes define a '50/50' relationship?

We cook – they eat; we clean – they dirty; we iron – they wrinkle.

How many blokes does it take to change a light bulb?

Four – one to carry the tool box, one to wear the utility belt, one to read the DIY manual and one to do the job.

How do you know when it's time to wash dishes and clean the house?

Look inside your pants; if you have a penis, it's **not** time.

How do you scare blokes?

Sneak up behind them and start throwing confetti.

How do you know when a bloke wants sex?

He's awake!

How do crazy blokes walk through the forest?

They take the psycho path.

How many blokes does it take to change a lightbulb?

Five. One to actually change the lightbulb and the rest to join him down the pub afterwards to moan about what a busy day he'd had!

How do you get a bloke to lift a feather duster?

Put it on top of the remote control!

How do blokes practise safe sex?

They meet their mistresses at least 50 miles from home.

How many blokes does it take to change a lightbulb?

At least two – one to climb the ladder and the other to tell him why he's doing it wrong!

How can you make sure your bloke doesn't make a fool of himself at a party?

Leave him at home.

How do you keep a bloke interested after marriage?

Wear perfume that smells like beer.

How can you tell that women have a sense of humour?

They get married.

5

SO THIS BLOKE GOES INTO A PUB...

This bloke walks into a bar on the top of a very tall building. He sits down, orders a huge beer, downs it in one, walks over to the window, and **jumps out**. Five minutes later, he walks back into the bar, orders another huge beer, downs it in one, walks over to the window, and **jumps out again**. Five minutes later, he

comes back and does the whole thing again. Not being able to contain his curiosity, another bloke at the bar stops him and says, 'I've got to ask how on earth are you doing that?!' The first bloke responds, 'Oh, it's simple physics, really. When you down the beer in one, it makes you all warm inside and since warm air rises, if you just hold your breath you become lighter than air and float down to the pavement.' '**Wow!**' exclaims the second bloke, '**I've got to have a go**'. So he orders a huge beer, downs it in one, goes over to the window, **jumps out**, and splats on the pavement below. The barman looks over to the first bloke and says, 'Superman, you're a **tosser** when you're drunk!'

This bloke goes into a pub followed by an **ostrich**. They both sit down and order two beers. Then the bloke reaches in his pocket and pulls out the exact money for the beers. Over the next few weeks they become regulars at the pub, always ordering drinks and paying with the correct change. The barman finally asks the bloke, 'How come you always have the right change?' The bloke replies: 'I found one of those magic genie bottles on the beach one day and made a couple of wishes. The first one was that I would always have the right amount of money to pay for anything I wanted.'

'That's ingenious,' says the barman. 'But what's with the ostrich?' 'Well,' says the bloke. 'I also wished for a **chick with long legs**.'

Two blokes are sitting at the bar and one says,

'I remember the first time I used alcohol as a substitute for women.'

'Yeah, what happened?' asked the other bloke.

The first bloke replies: 'I got my **knob stuck** in the neck of the bottle.'

This bloke's sitting in a pub, just looking at his drink. He stays like that for half-an-hour. Then a big tough-looking truck driver walks up to him, takes the drink, and swallows it all. The poor bloke starts crying.

The truck driver says: 'Come on, I was just joking. Here, I'll buy you another drink. I can't see a bloke crying.'

'No, it's not that,' says the bloke. 'This day is the worst of my life.

First, I overslept, and got to work late. My boss was furious, so fired me. When I left the building to go to my car, I found out it was stolen. Then the police said they couldn't do anything. I got a taxi home, and when I left the cab, I realised I'd left my wallet and credit cards in it. I got indoors and I found my wife in bed with the gardener. So I left home to come to this pub.

And just as I was thinking about putting an end to my life, you show up and drink my poison…'

A **bloke** walks into a pub and says, 'Give me two whiskies. One for me and one for my best mate.' The barman says, 'You want them both now or do you want me to wait until your mate arrives to pour his?' The bloke says, 'Oh, I want them both now. I've got my best mate in my pocket here.' He then pulls a little three inch man out of his pocket. The barman is amazed: 'Are you sure he can drink that much?' 'Of course,' says the bloke, you just watch. And with that the little man drank his whisky. 'What else can he do? Can he walk?' asks the barman. The man flicks a pound coin down to the end of the bar and says, 'Go on Bob, go and get the money.' The little man runs down to the end of the bar, picks up the pound coin, runs back down and gives it to the bloke. The barman's in total shock. 'That's amazing!' he says. 'What else can he do? Does he talk?' The bloke looks up at the bartender with a look of surprise in his eye and says: 'Talk? Sure he talks. Oi, Bob, tell him about that time we were in Africa on safari and you called that native Witch doctor an **asshole**!'

Two blokes are sitting in a pub and one is getting really depressed about the fact that his wife has left him. He keeps insisting that he's useless, but after a few pints his mate has convinced him he's better off without her. Then all of a sudden the dumped bloke bursts into tears. 'I don't even know what setting to use on the washing machine!' 'Oh, that's simple,' says the other bloke. 'What does it say on your shirt?' *'Arsenal.'*

A **couple are sitting in a bar** when the bloke notices an advert for alcopops showing a bare-chested hunk complete with six pack. 'Yeah, right,' says the bloke sarcastically. 'So if I drink ten bottles of that I'll look like him, will I?' 'No,' replies his girlfriend. 'When I drink ten bottles of that, **you'll** look like him!'

A bloke walks into a pub and asks the landlady for a double entendre. So she gives him one.

Two blokes go to the pub for their lunch. One of the blokes calls the waitress over and asks her for a quickie. Not surprisingly she slaps his face and storms off. Then his mate says to him: 'It's pronounced "quiche".'

6

IT'S A RELIGION THING!

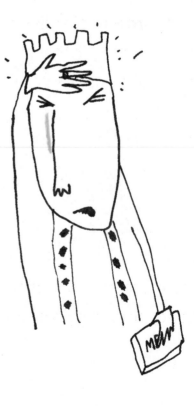

An old bloke goes into a Catholic Church and sits down in the confessional booth:

Bloke: 'I am 92 years old, have a wonderful wife of 70 years, many children, grandchildren, and great grandchildren. But yesterday I picked up two students who were hitchhiking. We went to a hotel, and I had sex with them three times.'

Priest: 'Are you sorry for your **sins?**'

Bloke: 'What **sins?**'

Priest: 'What kind of Catholic are you?'

Bloke: 'I'm not Catholic!'

Priest: 'Then why are you telling me all this?'

Bloke: 'I'm telling absolutely **everyone**!'

The **TRUE** story of creation...

In The Beginning, God created the **Heaven and the Earth.** And the Earth was without form, and void, and darkness was upon the face of the deep.

And the Devil said, 'It doesn't get any better than this.'
And so **God created Man** in His own image;
Male and female He created them.
And God looked upon **Man** and **Woman**
And saw that they were **lean and fit**.
And God **populated** the earth
With **broccoli** and **cauliflower** and **spinach**
And **green** and **yellow vegetables** of all kinds,
So **Man** and **Woman** would live long and **healthy** lives.
And so the Devil created **Fast Food Giants**.
And Fast Food Giants brought forth the **99p double cheeseburger**.
And the Devil said to Man, '**You want fries with that?**'
And Man said, '**Super-size them**.'
And Man **gained five pounds**.
And God said, '**Why** doth thou eatest thus?'
I have sent the **heart-healthy vegetables**
And **olive oil** with which to cook them.'
But the Devil brought forth **chicken fried steak**
So big it needed its own platter.
And Man gained **10 pounds**
And his **cholesterol** went through the roof.
And so God brought forth **running shoes**.

And Man resolved to lose **those extra pounds**.

And the Devil brought forth **cable TV** with **remote control**

So Man would not have to toil to **change channels** between **Sky Sports 1** and **Sky Sports 2**.

And Man gained another **20 pounds**.

And so God brought forth the **potato**,

A vegetable naturally low in fat and brimming with nutrition.

And the Devil peeled off the **healthful skin** and sliced the starchy centre into **chips** and deep-fat fried them.

And the Devil created **sour cream** dip.

And Man clutched his **remote control**

And ate the potato chips swaddled in **cholesterol**.

And the Devil saw and said, '**It is good**.'

And Man went into **cardiac arrest**.

And God sighed and created **quadruple bypass** surgery.

And the Devil cancelled Man's **health insurance**.

So God showed **Woman** how to peel the skin off chicken

And cook the nourishing **whole grain brown rice**.

And the Devil created **light beer**

So Man could **poison his body**,

While feeling righteous because he had to **drink twice as much** of the now-insipid brew to get the same buzz.

And Man gained another **10 pounds**.

And **Woman** ventured forth

Into the land of **chocolates**,
And upon returning asked Man, **'Do I look fat?'**
And the Devil said, **'Always tell the truth.'**
And **Man did**.
And Woman went out from the presence of Man
And dwelt in the land of the **divorce lawyer**,
East of the marriage counsellor.
And the Devil said, **'It really doesn't get any better
than this**.'

The three wise men arrived to visit the child lying in the manger. One of the wise men was exceptionally tall and bumped his head on the low doorway as he entered the stable. 'Jesus Christ!' he exclaimed.

Joseph said: 'Write that down, Mary; it's better than Clyde!'

Why did God make blokes first?

She wanted to start with something simple.

Dopey and the other seven dwarves are meeting the Pope at the Vatican. Dopey sidles up to him and says, 'Excuse me, Your Holiness, but **are there any dwarf nuns in Rome?**' The Pope thinks about it and says, 'No, Dopey, I don't think there are.'

Dopey shuffles from one foot to the other. '**Are there any dwarf nuns in the whole of Europe?**' Again, the Pope shakes his head.

Desperately now, Dopey says, '**Are there any dwarf nuns in the whole of the world?**' 'I'm sorry Dopey, but the answer is still no,' says the Pope. 'Why are you so concerned about this issue anyway?'

Shamefaced, Dopey points to the other six dwarves who are huddled in a corner, splitting their sides with laughter and chanting, '**Dopey shagged a penguin!**

A **boat is slowly sinking** and there's just one bloke left on board, praying. A lifeboat comes past and beckons him to jump on. 'No,' says the bloke. 'I have faith in the Lord. **God will save me**.'

The passenger continues to pray and suddenly a helicopter appears and throws down a rope. The pilot begs him to grab the rope but the bloke says: 'No, I have faith in the Lord. **God will save me**.' The boat continues to sink and the bloke continues to pray. Then a speedboat arrives, just as the boat is about to go down. But the bloke won't jump in and save himself. 'I have faith in the Lord,' he says. '**God will save me**.' Eventually the boat sinks and the bloke drowns. When he arrives in heaven he says to God: 'Lord, I trusted you all my life, but you let me down. I can't believe it.'

'You can't believe it!?' says God. '**And I sent you two bloody boats and a chopper!**'

7

SAY WHAT?

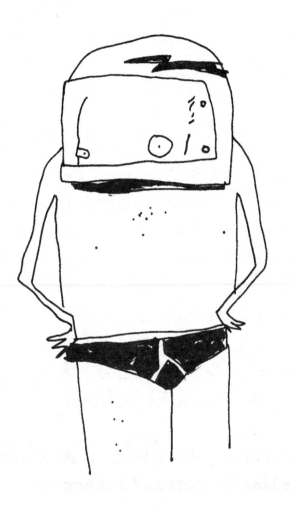

Bloke says: 'It's just **too hot** to wear clothes today, what do you reckon the neighbours would think if I mowed the lawn naked?'

New woman replies: 'Probably that I married you for your money.'

Bloke says: 'Shall we try swapping positions tonight?'

New woman replies: That's a good idea… you stand by the ironing board while I sit on the sofa and **burp**.'

Bloke says: 'This coffee isn't fit for a pig!'
New Woman replies: 'No problem. I'll get you some that is!'

Bloke says: 'When did you first realize you loved me?'
New woman replies: 'When I got upset at people saying you were ugly, fat and bloody useless!'

Bloke says:
'You know, I was
a fool when I married you.'
New woman replies:
'Yes, dear, but I
was in love and
didn't notice.'

Bloke says:
'Tonight I'm going
to make you the happiest
woman in the world.'
New woman replies:
'I'll miss you.'

Bloke says:
'Since I first
laid eyes on you,
I've wanted to make
love to you really badly.'
New woman replies:
'Well – you succeeded.'

Bloke says:
'Two inches more
and I'd be king!'
New woman replies:
'Two inches less,
and you'd be queen!'

Bloke says:
'Hey babe,
I'd sure love to get
into your pants.'
New woman replies:
'No thanks, I've already
got one arse in there.'

Bloke says:
'Will you tell me the
moment you orgasm?'
New woman replies:
'Only if you telephone!'

Bloke says:
'Haven't I seen you
someplace before?'
New woman replies:
'Yes, that's why I
don't go there anymore.'

Bloke says:
'Is this seat empty?'
New woman replies:
'Yes, and this one will
be if you sit down.'

Bloke says:
'Your place or mine?'
New woman replies:
'Both. You go to yours,
and I'll go to mine.'

Bloke says:
'Hey baby,
what's your sign?'
New woman replies:
'Do not enter.'

Bloke says:
'I'd go to the end of
the world for you.'
New woman replies:
'But would you
stay there?'

Bloke says:
'If I could see you
naked, I'd die happy.'
New woman replies:
'If I saw you naked,
I'd probably die laughing.'

Bloke says:
'Is there somebody else?'
New woman replies:
'Of course not.
Do you think I'd be
going out with an arse
like you if there was?'

8

WOMEN
ON TOP

A bloke left work one Friday afternoon, but being pay-day, instead of going home, he stayed out the entire weekend **partying with the boys** and spending his entire wage packet.

When he finally appeared at home on Sunday night, he was confronted by a **very angry wife** and was shouted at for nearly two hours about what a **rubbish husband** he was. Finally his wife stopped the **nagging** and simply said to him. 'How would you like it if you didn't see me for two or three days?'

'That would be fine with me,' said the bloke.

* * *

Monday went by and he didn't see his wife. Tuesday and Wednesday came and went with the same results. But on Thursday, the **swelling went down** just enough so he could see her a little out of the corner of his left eye.

A bloke is sitting next to a woman on the plane. To try to get her talking he asks if she'll play a game with him. She refuses, so he tries again. 'What if I ask you a question and if you get it wrong **you pay me a fiver**, then you ask me a question and if I get it wrong I pay you £50?' She agrees, as long as she can go first, then says '**What goes up a hill red and comes down it blue?**' And with that she turns over to sleep. The bloke looks puzzled and spends three hours searching the Web on his laptop for the answer. Eventually he wakes her with the £50 and admits defeat. Well, what is it?' With that she takes a fiver from her purse, gives it to the bloke and **goes back to sleep**.

A bloke is standing in the garden watching his wife cooking **burgers on the barbeque**. 'You know dear,' he says. '**Your bum is almost as wide as the grill** now!' She just pretends she can't hear him. Later in bed that night he tries to get a little friendly with her but **she pushes him away**. 'Darling, what's the matter, don't you want me?' the bloke says. 'No,' she replies 'I don't really think it's worth heating up this big grill for just **half a sausage** is it?!'

A **very attractive blonde** woman walks into a casino and says to the dealers: 'I want to bet everything I have on one throw of the dice, but in order to be lucky I have to **take off all my clothes**.' The dealers look at each other, **can't believe their luck** and agree that this will be fine. The **woman strips off** all her clothes, rolls the dice and then starts jumping up and down screaming '**Yes! I've Won!**', scoops up a huge pile of chips and her discarded clothes and leaves the casino. After a pause, one dealer turns to the other and says, 'So what did she throw?' The second dealer shrugs, 'I have no idea, I thought you were watching the dice'.

Moral: Blondes are not always stupid, but blokes are always blokes!

Did you hear about the woman who finally figured blokes out?
She **died laughing** before she could tell anybody.

A bloke went home to his wife with a present in his hand, but when she opened it, there was just a **tube of KY jelly**. 'That will **make you so happy** tonight!' said the bloke.
He was right! When he went out of the bedroom, she **squirted it all over the doorknobs** and he couldn't get back in.

This bloke decides that his missus **isn't paying him enough attention** in the bedroom, so he strips down to just his shoes and parades around in front of her saying, '**Notice anything special about me?**' To which she replies, '**No, not really**.' 'Come on,' he says. 'Look again. It's pointing to my shoes!' To which she replies, 'Pity you didn't **keep your hat on** instead then, isn't it?!'

First new woman: 'My ultimate fantasy is to have two blokes at once!'

Second new woman: 'Me too! One for cooking, the other for cleaning!!

There were two old women in the park, just enjoying the day when a man comes up to them and **exposes himself**. One woman **has a stroke**... but the other **couldn't reach**!

The bride, upon her engagement, went to her mother and said, '**I've found a bloke just like father!**' Her mother replied, 'So what do you want from me – sympathy?'

First new woman (proudly):

'My bloke's an angel!'

Second new woman:

'You're lucky, mine's still alive.'

Young girl:

'Is it true, mum? I heard that in some parts of Africa a woman doesn't know her husband until she marries him?'

Mum:

'That happens in every country, dear!'

A bloke lay dying. His wife, Becky, was maintaining a candlelight vigil by his side. She held his fragile hand, tears running down her face. Her praying roused him from his slumber. He looked up and his pale lips began to move slightly.

'**My darling Becky**,' he whispered.

'**Hush, my love**,' she said. 'Rest. Shhh, don't talk.'

But he was insistent. 'Becky,' he said in his tired voice, 'I have something I must confess to you.'

'There's nothing to confess,' replied the weeping Becky.

'Everything's all right, go to sleep.'

'No, no. I must die in peace, Becky. I… **I slept with your sister**, your best friend, her best friend, and your mother!'

'**I know**,' Becky whispered softly…

'**That's why I poisoned you**'

A **fireman comes** home from work one day and tells his wife. 'You know, we have a wonderful system at the fire station: **BELL 1** rings and we all put on our jackets, **BELL 2** rings and we all slide down the pole, **BELL 3** rings and we're on the fire truck ready to go. From now on when I say **BELL 1**, I want you to strip naked. When I say **BELL 2**, I want you to jump in bed. And when I say **BELL 3**, we're going to make love all night.'

The next night he comes home from work and yells '**BELL 1**!' His wife promptly takes all her clothes off. Then he yells '**BELL 2**!' His wife jumps into bed. When he yells '**BELL 3**!' they begin making love. After a few minutes his wife yells '**BELL 4**!'

'What the hell is **BELL 4**?' asks the bloke.

'Roll out more hose,' she yells, 'You're nowhere near the fire!'

Two women are discussing their blokes over coffee one day.

'You know,' says the first. '**My bloke eats like a pig**, drinks like a fish and is a rat as well. In fact he makes me so sick I can barely eat.

'Why don't you chuck him?' says the other woman.

'Well,' says the first. 'I just want to lose another 6lbs…'

A **bloke** and his wife have a bitter quarrel on the day of their **40th wedding anniversary**. The bloke yells, 'When you die, I'm getting you a headstone that reads:

"**Here Lies My Wife – Cold As Ever**".'

'Oh yeah?' she replies. 'Well when you die, I'm getting you a headstone that reads:

"**Here Lies My Husband – Stiff At Last**"!'

A female computer consultant was helping a smug bloke set up his computer and asked him what word he'd like to use as a *password* to log in with. Wanting to embarrass the woman he told her to enter **PENIS**.
Without blinking or saying a word she entered the bloke's *password* – and then almost died laughing at the computer's response:

*** *PASSWORD REJECTED. NOT LONG ENOUGH* ***

A **bloke** was reading the paper when an ad caught his eye: '**£500 Porsche! New!**' The bloke figured it had to be a joke as no-one would sell a new Porsche for £500, but thought it was worth a shot. He goes to the advertiser's house and sure enough, the woman was selling an almost brand new Porsche.

'**Wow!**' the bloke says. 'Can I take it for a test drive?'

The car runs perfectly – he can see no catch – but he's still suspicious.

'Why are you selling me this great Porsche for only £500?'

And the woman replies: 'My husband just ran off with his secretary, and he told me I could have the house and the furniture as long as I sold his Porsche and sent him the money.'

A **couple** are having a few problems and agree to see a marriage counsellor. When the counsellor asks the woman why she thinks the relationship is over, the woman replies simply: '***Because he's a lousy lover***.'

The counsellor then asks the bloke what he thinks of this, and the bloke replies: '***How can she tell in three minutes?***'

9

GREAT MYSTERIES OF OUR TIME (III) – WHY?

Why are gingerbread men the best men of all?

They're cute. They're sweet. And if they give you any lip you can bite their heads off.

Why don't blokes eat more M&Ms?

They're too hard to peel!

Why have **blokes** made such a **mess** of this world?

They're waiting for women to pick up after them.

Why is marrying a bloke like going to a restaurant with a group of friends?

You order what you want, then when you see what the other person has, you wish you'd ordered that.

Why do blokes take showers and not baths?

Because weeing in the bath would be disgusting.

Why are blokes blokes and rats rats?

Because rats had first choice.

Why can't a man be both handsome and intelligent?

Because that would make him a woman.

Why is a bloke's brain the size of a peanut?

Because it is swollen.

Why don't women get married so often these days?

Because they'd rather have bacon in the fridge than a pig in the living room.

Why is the bloke's intelligence worth more than the woman's?

It is rarer.

Why do blokes exist?

Who else is going to mow the lawn?

Why don't blokes go through menopause?

They never leave puberty.

Why do women close their eyes during sex?

They hate to see a
bloke enjoying himself!

Why won't women ever be equal to blokes?

Because they'll never walk
down the street with a
bald head and a beer gut and
still think they're beautiful.

Why aren't all blokes annoying?

Because some of them are dead.

Why do blokes like love at first sight?

It saves them a lot of time.

Why do blokes like blonde jokes?

Because they can understand them.

Why don't blokes have mid-life crises?

They're stuck in adolescence.

Why is the book
Women Who Love Too Much
a disappointment for blokes?

There are no phone numbers in it.

Why do blokes have
see-through lunch boxes?

So they can tell whether they're going to work or coming home again.

Why are computers
better than blokes?

They don't fart, they don't talk endlessly about footy, and they're always going down on you!

Why are blokes proof of reincarnation?

You can't get that dumb
in one lifetime!

Why do blokes with a pierced ear make the best boyfriends?

Because they're used to
pain and know how to
buy jewellery.

Why is it a waste of time telling a bloke to go to hell?

Because he'd get lost on the way.

10

IF MEN ARE
FROM MARS
AND WOMEN
ARE FROM
VENUS – BLOKES
ARE FROM
URANUS…

A bloke is walking down the beach and comes across an old bottle. He picks it up, pulls out the cork and **out pops a genie**.

The genie says, 'Thank you for freeing me from the bottle. In return **I will grant you three wishes**.'

The bloke says 'Great! I always dreamed of this and I know exactly what I want. First, **I want one billion dollars in a Swiss bank account**.' Poof!

There is a flash of light and a piece of paper with account numbers appears in the bloke's hand. He continues, 'Next, **I want a brand new red Ferrari** right here.' Poof! There is a flash of light and a bright red brand-new Ferrari appears right next to him. He continues, '**Finally, I want to be irresistible to women**.' Poof! There is a flash of light and he turns into a **box of chocolates**.

If one bloke can wash one stack of dishes in one hour, how many stacks of dishes could four blokes wash in four hours?

None. They'd all sit down together to watch the footy.

A bloke is staying in a hotel. 'And will there be anything else, sir?,' the bellboy asks after setting out an elaborate dinner for two. 'No thank you,' says the bloke, 'that will be all.' As the bellboy turns to leave he notices a beautiful satin **negligee** on the bed.

'Anything for **your wife**?' he asks.

'Oh yeah! That's a good idea,' the bloke says.

'Bring me a postcard.'

A bloke has been visiting Cuba for a week. He's leaving the next day and still hasn't **tried the local food**, so he goes to a restaurant and sits down to order, then sees the bloke next to him eating a delicious meal. Calling the waiter over he asks for the same meal, but the waiter says there's none left. The bloke asks him what it is and the waiter replies: '**That is the testicles from the bull that lost** the fight earlier that morning, if you come back tomorrow we'll save the dish for you.' So the bloke goes back the next day and the waiter has his food prepared for him. He eats the meal and calls the waiter over: '**This meal was delicious**, the only thing is it seemed a lot smaller than the one the bloke yesterday was eating.' And the waiter replies: **'Ah, sorry sir, sometimes the bull wins.'**

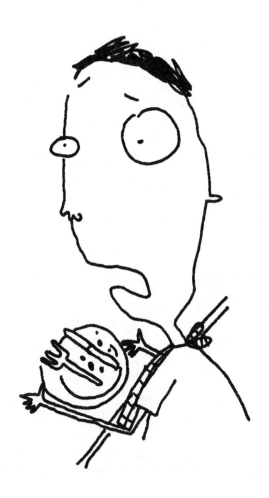

Two blokes were trying to get in a quick **18 holes of golf** but there were **two terrible women golfers** in front of them who were hitting the ball **all over the place** and **holding up the two blokes**. The first bloke says to his mate, 'Why don't you go over and ask if we can play through?' His mate agrees and gets about halfway over to the women, turns around sharpish and walks back to his mate. The first bloke says, '**What's wrong?**' His mate says, '**One of them is my wife and the other is my mistress**.' The first bloke says, 'Oh, that's a problem. I'll go over.' He too gets about halfway there, turns around and walks back. His mates says, 'What's wrong now?' The first bloke says, '**Small world.**'

A **drunk** is standing **peeing into a fountain** in the middle of town, so a **policeman** goes up to him and says: 'Stop that right now and put it away.' The drunk **puts his willy back into his trousers** and does up the zip. As the policeman turns to walk away the drunk starts to laugh. 'OK,' says the cop. '**What's so funny?**' 'Fooled you,' says the drunk. '**I may have put it away, but I didn't stop!**'

A **bloke** is sitting in the **first class section** on a plane to Africa but his ticket is only for **economy class** so the air hostess asks him to move. The bloke refuses, saying: 'I have a good job and pay all my taxes. **I deserve to sit in first class**.' After about 10 minutes of arguing the head air hostess comes and asks him to move. He refuses saying: 'I have a good job and pay all my taxes. I deserve to sit in first class.' After about another 10 minutes of arguing the pilot comes and whispers in the bloke's ear and he moves and sits at the rear of the plane. When the hostesses ask the pilot what he said, he answers: '**I told him the front half of the plane doesn't go to Africa**.'

In a transatlantic flight, a plane passes through a severe storm. The turbulence is awful, and things go from bad to worse when one wing is **struck by lightning**.

One woman in particular loses it. Screaming, she stands up in the front of the plane. '**I'm too young to die!**' she wails. 'But if I have to die, I want my last minutes to be memorable! I've had plenty of lovers in my life, but no-one has ever made me really feel like a woman! **Is there ANYONE on this plane who can make me feel like a WOMAN?**'

For a moment there's silence. Everyone has forgotten their own peril, and they all stare, riveted, at the desperate woman. Then a man stands up in the rear of the plane. '**I can make you feel like a woman**,' he says.

He's gorgeous. Tall, well-built, with long, flowing black hair and jet black eyes. He starts to walk slowly up the aisle, unbuttoning his shirt one button at a time. No-one moves. The woman is breathing heavily in anticipation as the stranger approaches. **He removes his shirt**. Muscles ripple across his chest as he reaches her, and extends the arm holding his shirt to the trembling woman, and whispers…

'**Iron this**.'

Grandpa was celebrating his **100th** birthday and everybody complimented him on how athletic and well-preserved he appeared.

'**Gentlemen, I will tell you the secret of my success**,' he cackled. 'I have walked for at least an hour in the open air day after day for some 75 years now.'

The celebrants were impressed and asked how he managed to keep up his rigorous fitness regime.

'Well, you see, my wife and I were married 75 years ago. **On our wedding night**, we made a solemn pledge. Whenever **we had a fight**, the one who was proved wrong would go outside and take a walk…'

A **couple** take their young son to the circus, and while the bloke's buying popcorn the boy asks: '**Mum, what's that long thing on the elephant?**'

'That's the elephant's trunk, dear,' she replies.

'No, mum. **Down underneath**.'

The woman blushes and says: 'Oh, that. That's nothing.'

The boy's dad returns, and his mum goes off to get a coke.

As soon as she leaves, the boy repeats his question.

'That's the elephant's trunk, son,' the bloke answers.

'Dad, I know what a trunk is. **What's the thing down there?**'

The bloke looks and says: 'Oh, that's the **elephant's penis**.'

'Dad,' the boy says. 'How come when I asked mum, she said it was nothing?'

The bloke takes a deep breath and explains: **Son, I've spoiled that woman**.'

When does a bloke open the car door for his wife?

a) when he's got a new car.
b) when he's got a new wife.

Once upon a time a female **brain cell** accidentally ended up in a **bloke's head**. She looked around nervously but it was all empty and quiet. '**Hello**?' she cried, but no-one answered.

'Is there anyone here?' she cried a little louder, but still no answer came. The female brain cell started to feel alone and scared and yelled: '**HELLO, IS THERE ANYONE HERE**?'

Then she heard a voice from far, far away: '**Hello, we're down here...**'

A **bloke is stranded** on a desert island with Pamela Anderson. Out of sheer loneliness the relationship becomes physical and for four months they enjoy **glorious sex**. Then one day the bloke says to her: 'Can I borrow your eyebrow pencil to **draw a moustache on you?**' 'I suppose so,' says Pamela. 'Would you wear some of my clothes and let me call you Bill?' he asks. Reluctantly she agrees. Then he grabs her by the arm and says: '**Hey Bill, you won't believe who I've been sleeping with** these last four months!'

A **bloke** gets home early from work and hears strange **noises coming from the bedroom**. He rushes upstairs to find his **wife naked on the bed**, sweating and panting. '**What's up?**' he says. '**I'm having a heart attack**,' cries the woman. He rushes downstairs to grab the phone, but just as he's dialling, his four-year-old son comes up and says 'Daddy! Daddy! Uncle Ted's hiding in your wardrobe and **he's got no clothes on!**' The bloke slams the phone down and storms upstairs into the bedroom, past his screaming wife, and rips open the wardrobe door. Sure enough, there's his brother, totally naked, cowering on the wardrobe floor. '**You rotten bastard**,' says the bloke. '**My wife's having a heart attack** and you're running around naked scaring the kids!'

A **married bloke** is having an affair with his **secretary**. One day, their passions overcome them and they take off for her house, where they make **passionate love all afternoon**. Exhausted from the **wild sex**, they fall asleep, awakening around 8.00pm. As the man throws on his clothes, he tells the woman to **take his shoes** outside and **rub them through the grass and dirt**.

Mystified, she nevertheless complies. He slips into his shoes and drives home. 'Where have you been!' demands his wife when he enters the house.

'Darling, I can't lie to you. **I've been having an affair** with my secretary, and we've been having sex all afternoon. I fell asleep and didn't wake up until 8.00pm.'

The wife glances down at his shoes and says, 'You lying bastard! **You've been playing golf!**'

A **bloke** was shipwrecked on a desert island for a whole year. Then one day a **stunning blonde** walks out of the sea dressed in scuba gear and lays down on the sand next to him. '**Would you like a cigarette?**' she asks. '**Of course**,' says the bloke – amazed as she unzips a pocket of the wetsuit, produces a pack of Marlboro, lights it seductively and passes it to him. '**How about a beer?**' she asks next. 'This is incredible,' says the bloke as she unzips another pocket of the wetsuit and produces a **chilled can of Stella** and two glasses, pouring them both a drink.

The blonde gets even closer to the bloke now and presses herself against him saying: '**And do you fancy playing around?**'

'Oh God,' says the bloke, thinking he's gone to heaven. '**Don't say you've got a set of golf clubs** in there too!'

A **bloke** spots a lamp by the roadside. He picks it up, rubs it vigorously, and suddenly **a genie appears**.

'I'll grant you **your fondest wish**,' says the genie.

The bloke thinks for a moment then says: 'I want a spectacular job – a job that no man has ever succeeded at or has ever attempted to do.'

'**Poof!**' says the genie. '**You're a housewife**.'

A **small boy** is lost at a large shopping mall. He approaches a uniformed policeman and says, '**I've lost my dad!**'

The policeman asks, '**What's he like?**'

And the little boy replies, '**Beer and women with big boobs.**'

11

WHAT ARE THEY LIKE?

Why are blokes like microwaves?

They both get hot in 15 seconds.

Why are blokes like dolphins?

They are both said to be intelligent, but no-one can prove it.

Why are blokes like video recorders?

They go forwards, backwards, forwards, backwards, stop and eject.

Why are blokes like a parking space?

Because all the best ones are taken and the rest are too small!

Why are blokes like chocolate?

The richer the better.

Why are blokes like a deck of cards?

You need a heart to love them, a diamond to marry them, a club to beat them and a spade to bury the bugger!

Why is a bloke like a clothes drier?

A 15 minute tumble and they're done.

Why are blokes like clouds?

**Eventually they
bugger off and
it's a really nice day!**

**Why are the best blokes
like toilet paper?**

Soft, strong and –
most of all –
disposable.

Why are blokes like decaffeinated coffee?

Neither of them will keep you going all night.